Tree Story

And Other Poems

Douglas G. Campbell

Oblique Voices Press | Portland, Oregon

Tree Story and Other Poems

Copyright © 2018 Douglas G. Campbell

ISBN-13: 978-0-9984446-1-1

*O*BLIQUE
VOICES PRESS

9310 SW 18th Pl
Portland, OR 97219

"Tree Story gives readers a point of entry into Douglas Campbell's unique connection with the earth. Taoist in its simplicity, Campbell's prose and poems show the potential for complex spiritual connections between human and tree, seed, soil, sun, wind, rock, and rain. Tree Story will touch you, leaving you with a deeper and more personal connection to your own natural world."

Lynn E. Fox, PhD, CCC-SLP
Associate Professor Emerita
Department of Speech & Hearing Sciences
Portland State University

"While most stories are told from the perspective of a single human, over some span of their life, this narrative is told from the perspective of a Douglas Fir with the wisdom and observation of a much longer view. You might think of this as the story of the social life of trees. We are allowed the vantage of sympathetic inter-species identification, by one called Quiet Hat. Sometimes it is worth listening to the quiet ones. On the other hand, Quiet Hat can fill the world with the sounds of a single forest eve."

Jay Beaman, PhD
Director of Institutional Effectiveness
Warner Pacific College

To all the ones who have done things for Quiet Hat....Rebecca, Joshua, and Ian.

Table of Contents

Foreword

I know Douglas Campbell best as a visual artist, and his work as a painter hangs in buildings across the campus where I teach, including what is probably my all-time favorite painting. It's a portrait of my mentor, a professor and colleague who first taught me to understand poetry. In some ways, having the honor of reading Doug's poetry feels like circle-of-life serendipity, my mentor's poetic sensibility providing me the tools I need to fully appreciate Doug's beautiful work.

Tree Story and Other Poems challenges us to see through a different lens, one that clarifies and sharpens the natural world, and that places humans as supporting actors in the grand drama nature gives us. The opening text, "Tree Story," beautifully traces the centuries-old life of a Douglas Fir, the tree itself narrating an epic journey with the action occurring at the tree's roots and around its trunk. After reading "Tree Story," I imagine I will never quite look at ancient forests the same way again.

Subsequent poems limn the theme established by "Tree Story": that is, we are called to celebrate life, even amidst the entropy and decay of a seemingly indiscriminate nature. For out of that entropy comes a fecundity that can serve as teacher, though we often do not attend to its lessons. Doug's astounding imagery in this collection yet calls us to learn, to see the natural world anew and to grow in understanding.

The collection's final work likens poetry to an orange, and we are invited to peel back its "tough rind," to taste its "juices," to know that it is good. *Tree Story and Other Poems* reflects well the simile Doug creates in this poem, the seeds he has planted here growing "in company/with earth and light."

Melanie Springer Mock, PhD
Professor of English
George Fox University

Tree Story

Guardian is my name according to the sign at my base. I have not always been named Guardian, but it is a name that fits me now. And now the other trees in my grove call me by the name Guardian. I have had other names during my long life of 542 years. My names have changed to fit the changes that have taken place in and around me.

But first, you need to know that my story comes to you as I have made it known to Quiet Hat. Quiet Hat is not his real name, but it is how I think of him, so it is the name I will call him. He has come here to my base, where my roots are anchored to earth. He is quiet, unlike most that come. I don't remember when he first came, but I know that he comes here often. And he comes when no others are here to intrude; he comes when it is cold, or in the early light of morning, or when the rain is heavy. He has come also at night in the darkness, when the moon is hiding. So I have given him my story that others might understand what it is like to be a tree, a very old Douglas Fir.

Like all of the other newly sprouted firs my first name was Seedling. We poked through the litter and bark of the forest floor. The Solomon's Plumes and ferns towered above us. I knew nothing of life then or just how fragile it could be. Small ticklers (you call them ants) clamored over and around us then. Larger, furry ticklers (you call them squirrels and chipmunks) brushed their long, soft tails against us as they dug and prodded the earth. Below the surface of the earth, among our fledgling roots were other creatures, the tube creatures (you call them worms). Most feared of those below the surface were the near-sighted diggers (you call them moles) who blundered and pushed. Many seedlings were undermined or uprooted. But I survived these early years.

Along with the other survivors, along with the others named Seedling, I was given a new name, Young One. The canopy of branches above blocked the light so the name Young One stayed with me for decades, until the great earthquake brought the elders, Broken Top, Tall One, the Fat Twins, tumbling down. Many of us Young Ones were crushed. Tower, one of the grandest of the elders almost crushed me. Tower fell within inches of my trunk and splintered many branches from my downhill side. Tower became my nurse log, feeding me while I prospered. I grew rapidly in this newly opened flood of light. I stretched upward and outward into the emptiness that earthquake had unfurled around me.

I became Tower's son as I fed upon his fallen strength. As Tower's son I gained a new perspective as each year I soared upward towards the light. Since sprouting I had felt a pounding of the earth deep down in my roots. But as I grew taller I could sense the mist that hung upon my branches. I could feel the winds pressing against my trunk and branches. I could taste the salt air that lay upon my needles. I began to learn of the ocean down below the slope on which I lived, how it pounded the land. Life was full of sameness and novelty.

Then one morning I felt pressure on my lower trunk. It was Long Braid. That is the name I gave him. Later I learned that others of his kind called him Raven Wing. I was used to sensing the animals that came and went.

Among them was the sure-footed Quiet One (deer, you call them). Washing Paws (or Raccoons) came often to hunt among the stones of rippling waters nearby. The fliers often flitted among my branches and some pounded my bark in search of ticklers. Some gray fliers built their nest among my branches and needles hatched their eggs, fed their young then flew away. But Long Braid's kind I had not seen before. Long Braid came softly, walking carefully between the others of the grove. Later he would bring Laughing Song. They did not come often, but when they did, smoke often rose up from the earth and strange aromas surrounded me. Long Braid came for many years, leaving shells and rounded sea stones to decorate the earth between my growing roots. He also brought the Lively Ones, the children he shared with Laughing Song. After the great fire he came only one more time, and he came alone.

Crackling fire came into our darkness after long months of dry and parching wind. First came the pain-filled screaming, filling my roots with dread. The presence of burning, falling and horror was passed from tree to tree as the flames rushed nearer. Many of the grove's smaller ones succumbed to the golden, licking fingers of death that sucked life from them. Flames beat against me, heat roasted air pounded and pummeled my bark. Smoke filled air brought me close to suffocation. I felt my life evaporating from each cell within me. But I did not die; I did not fall to become nurse to future seedlings, though some day I will. This fire continued up the slope and past the ridge top above and behind me. And I was alone.

The remains of Tower, my nurse and sustainer were ashen and black. The grove was gone leaving me alone with my pain and my grief. My grove was gone and I wished that I too had burned. Then Long Braid came after the first rains of autumn. He wept at the scarred base of my scabbed and invalid trunk. He said good-bye for the last time, and then he too was gone forever. Pain and loneliness wrapped me in a cocoon of death from which I believed no radiant butterfly could emerge. But soon fireweed and small creatures, those that had hidden deep within the cool earth, emerged. Some fled in search of some distant grove painted with green. Others stayed behind as life rose up from the earth, fed now by mist and rain. My new name became Survivor.

As fireweed flourished and salal began to sprout green shoots from remnants that did not perish, the skeletons of my grove continued to haunt me. Why did I live while all those around me succumbed to those killer flames? Soon, winter winds pushed ashore and rain undermined dead roots. I remember that winter, it still returns to my dreams as the winter of the falling ones. On dark nights or on brightly lit days after rainstorms or after the mist turned to ice they fell, came crashing down around me. My stiff and lifeless brethren: Mist Clinger, Wide Crown, and Wind Cutter came tumbling to the earth, sending shock waves of pain to prod and pierce the cloak of denial that I had wrapped around my fear and anger. Why did my grove have to die; every one except me?

There were times deep in that winter of the falling ones that I wanted to give in to the winds, let go my grip on soil and stone, to come diving down. There were times when I had given in to despair, but my roots were strong and held in spite of my desire. And my scarred bark began to heal. Crows and gulls came to my branches; bats flung their high-pitched sight into my surrounding night and butterflies again danced in the sun. As life returned to me I turned back to life. When spring returned, a carpet of sprouts spread green across the land. I was no longer alone for the grove had been born anew at my base. I had been spared, I came to believe, to pass on the knowledge of the grove to these new ones those small bits of life I now called Seedling. I quickly abandoned my name Survivor and became Loving Mother for all the seedlings of my grove.

For the next century as Loving Mother, I nurtured these seedlings, spread my limbs over them as they grew and struggled and prospered. Not all of my seedlings survived. Many were lost to drought or wind or ice. But my grove has been reborn; my slope is covered not just with firs, but also with cedars, and maples and spruce. The waves below pounded out the time through days and weeks and years. And many hundreds of tides have washed in and out, down below my grove, at the base of my slope. I have left my loneliness behind and I have become part of a new grove along with Slender Trunk, Bird Keeper, Gray Bark and others.

But these calm times of growth did not last forever. My flourishing grove was cracked with percussive explosions. Big Antlers, his cows and calves beat the forest floor with their hooves. Next came the barking dogs, overheated and slobbering at the hooves of the youngest calf, a newborn elk. Big Antlers charged the dogs and tossed these barking hounds against my trunk. Then there came more percussive explosions. Red blotches appeared on Big Antlers shoulder. He trumpeted loudly as his family crossed the ridge above, then his legs crumpled and he fell. There he lay, sprawled across my roots, wilted and coughing, exhaling blood. I held him with my roots and sought to soothe him as he slowly died.

Shouting ones were soon upon him; they came to flay this fallen, dying elk. For months afterwards I cradled the bones they left. I became the altar for this bloody sacrifice tossed away without honor by the shouting ones. There was no grace, no reverence; bones were flung aside as flesh was stripped away. For many decades, anger dwelt within my core, and I came to hate the shouting ones. Long Braid had taken the deer with his silent arrows. But before flesh was cut away from bone, Long Braid thanked the deer for its sacrifice, and then Long Braid thanked the earth. Each time Long Braid killed it was with a reverent precision. He filled every move, every gesture of his hands with awe for the life he took.

More shouting ones came cracking the air, sending all those that dwelt below into headlong flight. But, worse than the shouting ones, were the cutters. The cutters sawed and chopped their way through to the edge of my grove. They flattened the earth and brought their machines to slash roads then covered them with ground stones. Then trucks came to haul away the fallen victims. For reasons I do not understand, most of my grove was spared. Even now, the screaming blades, the stink of petroleum fumes and the reverberations following each crashing tree brought down to death remain with me, nightmares come to life. These deaths, this pogrom led to new life, but the pain of this cutting I hold in my memory, a scar that has healed but that has not been discarded.

More stench came. Asphalt flowing over ground stones burning and searing the earth's skin. Nameless moles, worms, shrews, beetles, and ants were crushed unto death. In place of ferns, bracken, moss, lilies, salmon berries and much more, there is now a slab of blackness. Cars and trucks groan by, shredding the veil of quiet and order that had once been suspended throughout the night. Flashing metallic colors speed past, seldom stopping except to expel cans, or bottles, or bags of refuse into the shocked silence of our grove. Our peace is in constant jeopardy, unraveled day and night. Fumes burn through the air binding allergies to all our inhalations.

Since then, a black path has snaked upwards between the trunks and come to a halt at my base. People come when there is no rain or snow. The old ones, breathing heavily, rest upon the bench. They tilt back their heads and gaze upon me before they turn and leave. The small ones clamor over my roots and hide among the fluted flanges of my base shouting and giggling. It is only when they look upward that they too become silent, if only for a moment. These small ones grasp my trunk like they do the legs of their parents. I hope that they will not become shouters or cutters. Below me now is a sign that gives me the name Guardian. I have become the Guardian of my grove. My age and my size bring some protection to my grove. I recognize some of the people that come back time after time to visit me—those that bring others to my base to stare at me—they would not suffer me to be cut nor the other of my grove that surround me.

I have given the knowledge of my names and of my life to Quiet Hat for he is the one who now knows me best.

He brings his small ones with him, both of them boys—I call them Dark Hair and Bright Hair. Bright Hair likes to play his imaginary trumpet and twirl, dancing about my trunk. Dark Hair is quieter, he likes to touch me; he likes to search the deep ridges of my trunk. With Quiet Hat, Dark Hair and Bright Hair also comes Quiet Reader. Quiet Reader often brings a book to read in silence upon the bench below me. She reads then thinks, looks up at my branches, and then reads again. It is strange to know that the pages of her book and the pages that you now read are made from the fibers of my own kind.

I talk about Quiet Hat and his family; I talk of Long Braid and others for they have shown me that not all humans are shouters and cutters. They have shown me that not all humans look at me and think of the number of houses that could be built from my body. They do not look at the gentle slopes where I dwell with my grove and think, "what a wonderful place to develop into one-acre home sites, but of course most of these old trees would have to go." I know as my thoughts enter Quiet Hat his thoughts also enter me. As I have told Quiet Hat my story he has told me his. I am very old and may have gained some wisdom. My message to Quiet Hat and to you is simple "choose life."

and other poems...

Soil

When I stand barefoot
in the grass
roots attach themselves
to my toes
to the soles of my feet
my heart draws up water
from the soil
absorbs nutriments
minerals blend with oxygen
within blood cells
buds form at my fingertips
my skin becomes hard
barklike in texture
cellulose stiffens my brain
I no longer think
birds perch on my shoulders
squirrels leave acorns
in my ears
the sun warms my growing
sap oozes through my pores
I stand still and rest
as the earth recharges my brain
so that I may walk
quietly again

Sharing the Sun

Small, reddish, maple branches stretch,
reach up into the drizzle
that was earlier snow, when the ground
and street were made white.
The green, then yellow,
leaves of the maple left
months ago. They fell or
fluttered, then drifted with the wind
until the rain glued them together
into a mouldering mat.
 By spring the mat first yellow,
then brown, will have melted,
at least in part, and new leaves,
first light yellow-green,
then darker, will fill
the reddish branches.
Then once again, the fir and cedar
will have to share the sun.

Blowdown

Undulate regiments,
tall firs carpeting
the ridges as they surge
toward promontories of stone
yet unconquered.
Spruce sentinels patrol
the perimeters where scree
and trunks collide.

Battalions of wind
lead the counterattack,
scattering wooden shafts
like pick-up sticks,
predicting futures of death
to the shallow rooted
conifers not well entrenched.
Acres of confusion
tangled by the winter wind's deceit
leave only one tall fir
standing alone,
leaning into the darkness,
held aloft not by power of root age
but by the fallen.

When spring's fountain of melt water
undermines squirrels, borrowings
and weary roots—
all would fall down,
if only the skeletons
would loose their talons,
unloose their grip,
and grant release

and let fall this monument,
this hollow corpse
bound in isolated death.

Stone

I lie upon a rock
my joints freeze
lichens grow on my shoulders
veins of silver
slide between muscles
a lizard crawls
from my mouth
to lie in the sun's warmth
upon my skull
I am quiet
I become still
my mind is at total rest
 the strength of the earth
fills the crystals
that once were blood
my eyes stare blindly
ants file along my spine
crickets begin to dance
tickling my feet
soon my blood will wake again
then I must rise
and separate myself
from the earth

Night Listeners

I fill my canvas pack
with a wind full of sounds
a wind which binds the earth within
its choreography of clouds
drawing out the voices of many singers who
have buried deep within their minds
psalms forgotten by the tired ear
I am the listener

and though I have not a perfect pair of ears
ears which only God can have
I am patient enough to wait the night
to hear the dry scraping
of the lizard's foot across the hemlock's bark

I sink into the amniotic juices
between the argument of reeds
which face the water
to hear frog's belching at the night's reflection
I slither through the evening's pastures
between the naked seed filled pods
collecting parched conversations in the grass
the persistent circadian percussion
that blinds the tender ear

at the wood's edge where trees divide the sky
I listen for the cautious feet, which cling
to the flying squirrel's scrabbling hunt
while below among the crippled rhododendron
intrudes an unafraid waddling gait
reeking with the tarnished breath of skunk

I am never seen as I hide between the stars
collecting the shiny beetles' stumblings
and the ripping, dying cries which scatter
the dead ashes of night's shroud
multiple threads stitching up the quilted sounds
woven by the thumping owl in flight
or the needled claws of the amber lynx

warnings too late to save the gnawing mice
foraging within the quiet hidden pockets of the moon
I gather the haunted laughter
pines creaking whining, moaning with delight
branches sharing secrets with the wind

I sweep up all the small sounds
all the light feathered whispers found
beneath the leaves among the fern
from the stream's narrow envelope I unfold
the constant rattle of the rocks
the tiny strings of sounds threaded
without cadence through continuous needles
sharp bright tones which I cannot sing

I crowd the flickering ring of light
which campfires burn into the black
to watch the crackling, hissing flame lapping
at concentric diaries of oak

In the deep intervals, before morning light
when all the gleaming pools of sound
have been siphoned off and swallowed
when the pond is emptied of its croaking
and the brittle wings of cicada are still and
only a hollow silence surrounds night's throat

when mist clings to the cold hanging above the water
and the wild putti have folded up their wings and
ceased dancing through the night

all is asleep or waiting for the sun
leaving only quiet for the listener
I glue the sounds stolen from my searching
upon the withered pages of my albums
where they lie limp as an empty dress
on a dusty wooden floor without footsteps

The Customs of the Moon

I am no astronomer.
My parents never taught me
the customs of the moon;
when she will bring the waters of the sea
flowing up into the estuaries of salt
or let the tides flow back
into the recessed throats of oceans.

The legends which regulate the winds
never reached for my ears
never taught my brain how to read
the leaves that fall from trees.
I cannot measure the winter's tides
within the thickness of an oak tree's bark
or gauge the coming storm's intent
from the crests and troughs
which tumble through the fields of grass.

I am often scoured by rain
which earlier clouds did not predict,
or swept away by unseen currents
which break the surface image of glass,
or left in some eddy up against a rock
trapped by my lack of strength.

The seasons change before I notice
that ice is forming around the eyelids
or that frost has turned my beard to white.
Seasonal rains cut ravines in the skin,
erosion takes its grinding route
plowing furrows beneath my eyes.
Forests recede from the upper slopes

leaving the mountain's skull exposed.

I have not learned that valleys
hold the easiest paths to dreams.
High mountains act as magnets
drawing breaths from lungs,
attaching vices to the calf muscles.
No shaman ever drove the wings
of hawks from my retinas,
nor hung an amulet of stone around my neck,
nor forced me to drink the valley's brew
to drive away the ghosts of falling
from the nightmares of my climbs.

I can never foresee when the summit
will be hidden by stone dense mist
or when the green-eyed moon
will wash the open sky with night.

Seeds

Like an orange
poetry
has a tough rind
holding in the juices,

juices which dance
upon the tongue
and cradle seeds,

seeds that grow
in company
with earth and light.

Acknowledgements:

Thank you to the editors of the following publication in which this poem first appeared:

The Path: A Literary Magazine: "Earthsleep"

Thank you to the following people who contributed to this book:

Amber Kirkwood, for her help editing, publishing and book cover design for both Tree Story and Turning Radius.

Lynn Fox, for her contribution of the photo *Hawthorn,* which appears on the cover of Tree Story.

Caleb Clayton for his help in formatting the manuscript for printing.

Andrea Roberts, for her help with arranging book design files for Tree Story.

Other books by Douglas G. Campbell:

Turning Radius: A Book of Poetry. (Portland, Oregon: Oblique Voices Press, 2017)

Facing the Light: The Art of Douglas Campbell. (Portland, Oregon: Oblique Voices Press, 2012)

Parktails. (Eugene, Oregon: Wipf and Stock Publishers, 2012)

Seeing: When Art and Faith Intersect. (Lanham, Maryland: University Press of America, 2002).

About the Author:

Douglas G. Campbell lives in Portland, Oregon. He is Professor Emeritus of art at George Fox University where he taught painting, printmaking, drawing and art history courses. His poetry and artworks have been published in a number of periodicals, and his artwork is represented in collections such as The Portland Art Museum, Oregon State University, Ashforth Pacific, Inc. and George Fox University.

Tree Story and the poems in this book were written throughout the years before his stroke in 2012, which subsequently left him with a language disorder called aphasia. This book reflects the process of reengaging with his former writing and also encouraging him to share his work with the world.

Reflection by the author November 2017:

The author's words as dictated to his wife, Rebecca while he read *Tree story.*

"There are things that are good and are bad, and there are things that are black. This road is coming through and it interrupts all things. I am a guardian and they come to greet me and I feel good. I like them. Dark Hair and Bright Hair are two boys. (Joshua and Ian). Bright Hair frolics around my trunk. That is one kind. And Dark Hair is different. The touch of my trunk and head are something that makes me happy. Dark Hair and Bright Hair come with Quiet Reader. You are Quiet Reader, Rebecca, I am always Quiet Hat."

"Friends are you, Rebecca and they have been working with me to say things that I don't say. I wonder if this is enough."

www.ingramcontent.com/pod-product-compliance
Lightning Source LLC
Chambersburg PA
CBHW030309030426
42337CB00012B/651